D0572482

MAN AND MONUMENT

By FRANK FREIDEL

Professor of History, Harvard University

and

LONNELLE AIKMAN

National Geographic Senior Editorial Staff

WASHINGTON NATIONAL MONUMENT ASSOCIATION

with the cooperation of the National Geographic Society

WASHINGTON, D. C.

COVER: *Unfinished portrait of George Washington, painted from life in 1796 by Gilbert Stuart.*
COURTESY BOSTON ATHENAEUM, ON DEPOSIT AT THE BOSTON MUSEUM OF FINE ARTS

FRONT ENDSHEET: *Throngs cheer Washington's victorious re-entry into New York City on November 25, 1783, in this 1850 lithograph.*
COURTESY JANICE E. CHRABAS

FRONTISPIECE: *Portrait of Washington, painted by Charles Willson Peale in 1779, shows him as commander in chief of the Continental Army.*
COURTESY PENNSYLVANIA ACADEMY OF THE FINE ARTS

TITLE PAGE: *The Washington family coat of arms bears a 15th-century spelling in its scroll. The name probably evolved from de Wessington, which appears in earlier English records.*
LIBRARY OF CONGRESS

WASHINGTON NATIONAL MONUMENT SOCIETY
(Founded 1833)

Lyndon B. Johnson	President ex officio
Governors of the states	Vice Presidents ex officio
Ulysses S. Grant 3rd	First Vice President
John Lord O'Brian	Second Vice President
Charles Carroll Glover, Jr.	Treasurer
George B. Hartzog, Jr.	Secretary

MANAGERS: Hon. Earl Warren, Melville Bell Grosvenor, Frederick M. Bradley, Senator Harry Flood Byrd, Colgate W. Darden, Jr., Hon. Charles S. Dewey, David E. Finley, George Hamilton, Jr., Adm. Thomas C. Kinkaid, Dr. Cloyd Heck Marvin, Benjamin M. McKelway, Samuel Spencer, Corcoran Thom, Jr.

MANAGERS EMERITUS: Gilbert H. Grosvenor, Samuel H. Kauffmann, Adm. C. R. Train

WASHINGTON NATIONAL MONUMENT ASSOCIATION

Ulysses S. Grant 3rd	President
John Lord O'Brian	Vice President
George B. Hartzog, Jr.	Secretary
Corcoran Thom, Jr.	Treasurer
Cornelius W. Heine	Assistant Secretary
William H. Hamilton	Assistant Treasurer

Produced by the Special Publications Division of the National Geographic Society as a public service

STAFF FOR THIS BOOK

Melville Bell Grosvenor	Editor in Chief
Franc Shor	Editorial Director
Robert L. Breeden	Editor
Donald J. Crump	Assistant Editor

Text by Frank Freidel and Lonnelle Aikman

Bruce Brander, Barbara Coulter, Barbara J. Hall, Geraldine Linder, Robert C. Magis, Margaret McKelway, Mary Anne McTaggart, Charlene L. Murphy, Patricia G. Rosenborg, Margaret C. Shaw, James R. Whitney

Copyright © 1965 by the WASHINGTON NATIONAL MONUMENT ASSOCIATION, a nonprofit affiliate of the Washington National Monument Society, chartered on March 30, 1965. Headquarters: Room 776, 1800 G Street, N. W., Washington, D. C. 20006

Library of Congress catalog number 65-25573

PRESS OF JUDD & DETWEILER, INC., WASHINGTON, D. C.
COLOR PLATES BY LANMAN ENGRAVING CO., ALEXANDRIA, VIRGINIA

COMMEMORATIVE *medallion celebrates laying of the cornerstone of the Washington Monument, July 4, 1848.*

The ceremony fulfilled a pledge made 65 years earlier by the Continental Congress to honor George Washington.

Reverse side of the medal shows structure as designer Robert Mills originally conceived it—an obelisk 600 feet high, growing from a circular colonnaded base.

SMITHSONIAN INSTITUTION

Foreword

EACH FAMILY has its folklore, and my own was no exception. Quite early in life I learned about my mother's grandfather, George Washington Baines, and how he lived up to the challenge of that proud name by becoming a preacher and educator. Likewise, I heard a great deal about a raw frontier settlement called Washington-on-the-Brazos, where my great-granduncle met with other pioneers in March, 1836, to sign the Texas Declaration of Independence.

Many Americans have similar recollections, for the name of George Washington follows us through life like a close relative. Our maps show streets, cities, mountains, lakes, and even a great western state named Washington. Our youngsters learn their ABC's beneath a portrait of our first President. We print his image on our stamps and mint his profile on coins.

Most of all, we remember him on the banks of the river where he caught his herring, tilled his crops, and planted his trees, his own "Potomack." Across it and upstream from "my Vine and Fig tree," as he called Mount Vernon, stands a place "not excelled for commanding prospect, good water, salubrious air, and safe harbour by any in the world." His countrymen made it the greatest of the cities named Washington. And its tallest spire is the obelisk we call the Washington Monument. This book tells its story.

But more than that is told within these pages. Scholars say we can judge a people by the men they honor. The man who was George Washington explains something about his American heirs.

We see him here as a young surveyor, as a frontier explorer, as a soldier, farmer, and a statesman: always strong, honorable, methodical, a man of truly heroic endurance.

He loved life, yet willingly risked it, for he held duty dear.

One of my favorite stories of George Washington is about his political campaign for the Virginia House of Burgesses when he was only 26. He was on duty with his troops at Fort Cumberland. Nervous friends back home urged him to "come down and show your face." One even warned that "being elected absolutely depends on your presence." Washington ignored the political advice, did his duty—and won the election.

Throughout his life, glory pursued the man. Because he worked hard at his duty, George Washington won independence for our hard-pressed people. As the first President of an insecure nation, he brought it an essential unity. We sometimes forget today that President Washington had to make hard, controversial decisions. His own words remind us of the task; these were written in 1798 after his retirement:

"To expect that all men should think alike . . . would be to look for a change in the order of nature; but at so dangerous a crisis as the present, when every thing dear to Independence is at stake, the well disposed . . . might, one would think, act more alike. . . .

"But I will unite with you in a fervent wish, and hope, that greater unanimity than heretofore, will prevail . . . and that, the young men of the present day will not suffer the liberty for which their fore fathers fought, bled, and died, and obtained [to] be lost by them; either by supineness, or divisions among themselves. . . ."

Every President since Andrew Jackson has been ex officio President of the Washington National Monument Society. The office is ceremonial and the burden light. But like that view of the Monument itself from the President's Office in the White House, it reminds us of a hero and a duty.

CAPTURED IN LIFE—*George Washington at 53. Commissioned by the General Assembly of Virginia to prepare a statue of Washington "of the finest marble and the best workmanship," French sculptor Jean Antoine Houdon arrived at Mount Vernon in October, 1785. After making a plaster life mask, Houdon cast from it two clay busts, one of which (above) remains at Mount Vernon.*

The years had been full ones for the Virginia planter. As a young man Washington enjoyed the refined and sophisticated colonial atmosphere into which he was born. He had also faced the dangers of frontier life during the French and Indian War.

When at 43 he accepted command of a raw Continental Army fighting for independence, he could not have imagined the hardships he would face before victory came six years later.

Now, in middle age, a weary Washington sought retirement from public service at his home on the Potomac River. But his country would again call him into action. In 1789 he would take on the task of building a government. The man first in war would become first in peace.

T HE WEATHER was glorious in Washington on the Fourth of July, 1848. As a local newspaper reported, "... a heavy rain, falling in the early part of the previous day, had cooled the earth and the air, and ... seemed gladly to lend its aid to the joy and grandeur of the occasion."

The occasion was indeed significant, for the Nation's Capital was about to celebrate Independence Day by watching the laying of the cornerstone for the memorial we know as the Washington Monument.

Behind the work begun in that long-ago time stood an organization called the Washington National Monument Society. Founded in 1833, it still exists. And as its current First Vice President,* I take particular satisfaction in introducing this book. For in it you find not only tribute to the genius of George Washington, but the dramatic and little-known story of the creation of a memorial worthy of that genius.

From the beginning, the public was intensely interested in Washington's Monument. At the cornerstone laying, a huge crowd—drawn from the hinterlands as well as the city—gathered for the ceremony. Among the audience moved scores of outstanding leaders of Federal, state, territorial, and civil governments, representatives of military and fraternal organizations—even Indian chiefs from western tribes.

Benjamin B. French, Grand Master Mason of Washington, was on hand to con-

*By law, the President of the United States is the Society's President.

Introduction

secrate the cornerstone with traditional rites, in which he would use the same trowel that Washington himself had used in laying the Capitol's cornerstone 55 years before.

But first the Hon. Robert C. Winthrop of Massachusetts, Speaker of the House of Representatives, delivered the day's chief address. In the oratorical style of the period, he praised Washington's character and many services to his country.

"Proceed, then, fellow citizens," he said in closing. "Lay the cornerstone of a monument which shall adequately bespeak the gratitude of the whole American people. . . . Build it to the skies; you cannot outreach the loftiness of his principles!"

In the biographical section of the book, you read of events that shaped George Washington's life and prepared him for his future crucial leadership.

Though born to the relative comfort of 18th-century Virginia plantation society, young Washington dared the rigors of frontier exploration and strife. Defying the British throne, he took the risks, in the Revolution, of being killed or hanged as a traitor. As the first President of a weak republic in a world of strong, hostile monarchies, he found that "every thing, *in our situation* will serve to establish a Precedent," and added, characteristically, "it is devoutly wished . . . that these precedents may be fixed on true principles."

After Washington's death, it was not easy for the American people to decide on and carry through a permanent testimonial that would match the measure of the man.

How the goal was achieved in the towering Washington Monument forms the theme of the major portion of this volume.

The story covers a full century. Including false starts, political turmoil, and even thieves who made off with part of the Monument, it runs from the Administration of Washington's successor, John Adams, to that of Chester A. Arthur. While the shaft was under way, the Nation went through the agony of a civil war, and transformed itself from a farm and pastoral land to one well along on the surging stream of industry.

The Washington Monument Society is deeply grateful to Dr. Melville Bell Grosvenor, President and Editor of the National Geographic Society, for the preparation of *Washington, Man and Monument*.

The Geographic's editorial and photographic staffs have turned out a highly readable and lavishly illustrated work. Produced as a public service, it follows similar publications on the United States Capitol, the White House, and the American Presidents.

The Monument and Geographic Societies are linked by old ties of friendship, strengthened by long and active membership in the Monument group by both Melville Grosvenor and his father, the Geographic's former President and Editor, Dr. Gilbert H. Grosvenor.

As one who has long supported efforts to honor the memory of George Washington, I am delighted to see this book offered to the public as a notable contribution to better understanding and appreciation of our first President.

ULYSSES S. GRANT 3rd
First Vice President
Washington National Monument Society

The Life of George Washington

By FRANK FREIDEL

GEORGE WASHINGTON, as generations of school children have been taught, was the Father of his Country, and, in the words of Henry Lee, "first in war, first in peace, and first in the hearts of his countrymen." Olympian among Presidents, Washington even in his own lifetime was almost obscured as a person by the awe-inspiring legend enveloping him. But behind the legend stands an impressive human being who, foremost among the Founding Fathers, wrought a new United States and guided it through its first years.

Decades of training prepared Washington for his leadership in the Revolution and the establishment of the new Republic. Born in 1732 into a planter family in Virginia, Washington received from his parents and half brothers schooling in the morals, manners, and body of knowledge requisite for an 18th-century Virginia gentleman. His birthplace at Wakefield is commemorated with a reconstructed brick mansion on the original plantation site, now a national monument.

In his youth, Washington pursued two intertwined interests that gave direction to much of his life—military arts and western expansion. War was almost a normal condition in those days, as the rivalry between England and France erupted intermittently into lengthy conflict. Washington's half brother Lawrence served in an expedition against Cartagena in Colombia, one of the possessions of the French ally, Spain, and named his estate on the Potomac in honor of the commander, Adm. Edward Vernon. In time, Washington acquired the property and retained the name, Mount Vernon.

At 16 Washington helped survey Shenandoah lands for Thomas, Lord Fairfax. Thereafter he spent much of his life in the saddle, surveying or soldiering in the wilderness.

In 1753, when French soldiers trespassed on lands claimed by Virginia in the Ohio country, Governor Robert Dinwiddie sent the 21-year-old Washington to warn them away. The following year, commissioned a lieutenant colonel, he fought the first skirmishes in what grew into the French and Indian War. The French defeated Washington and his force of about 300 men, and in 1755 surrounded and routed the British reg-

YOUNG WASHINGTON holds a surveying instrument while his companion pays out chain to fix distance. At 14 Washington surveyed his neighbors' fields. At 16 he plotted Lord Fairfax's lands, sleeping under "one thread Bear blanket with double its Weight of Vermin...." His surveyor's office at his father's Ferry Farm estate near Fredericksburg, Virginia, is open to the public. Wakefield, the farm on which Washington was born, is now a national monument.

GIANT OF HIS TIME, Washington stood six feet two and weighed 200 pounds. Gilbert Stuart's portrait is the only object in the White House that has been there since its occupancy in 1800. Dolley Madison in 1814 delayed her flight from the invading British until she safeguarded the canvas.

ENGRAVING BY G. R. HALL FROM A PAINTING BY F. O. C. DARLEY, LIBRARY OF CONGRESS (ABOVE) AND WHITE HOUSE COLLECTION © N.G.S.

LIBRARY OF CONGRESS

MYTH GILDS THE BOYHOOD YEARS *of America's first citizen. The famous cherry tree legend (illustrated above) depicts a repentant George freely admitting he tried to cut down his father's favorite tree. But the story first appeared in 1806 —seven years after Washington's death—in a biography of Washington written by clergyman and bookseller Mason Locke Weems.*

Wakefield (right), his modest birthplace overlooking Popes Creek in Westmoreland County, Virginia, vanished in 1779. The plantation endures as a national monument, but the house now occupying the site is a copy of a farm dwelling of the period, as is the homestead seen in this artist's conception.

But other stories from the early life of George Washington have roots in fact. In a scene (below), keen disappointment clouds the boy's face as he yields to his mother's pleas and gives up hope of pursuing a career in the navy. His younger brothers and sister witness the episode.

MAKESHIFT RAFT, *fashioned with "one poor Hatchet," carries George and his guide Christopher Gist into the wintry Allegheny River. In 1753, Washington volunteered for an official mission to French Fort LeBoeuf in Ohio country. His duty: to warn the French to get off the British-claimed land; to reconnoiter the fort's military situation; and to win to Britain any Indians encountered. Here, on the return journey, ice floes endanger the travelers, who shortly had to "quit our Raft" and swim to an island.*

LIBRARY OF CONGRESS

LIBRARY OF CONGRESS

ulars under Gen. Edward Braddock. Washington, an aide to Braddock, escaped injury, although four bullets ripped his coat and two horses were shot from under him.

For several years thereafter, as a colonel commanding a force of only 300 Virginians, he undertook the difficult task of defending a 350-mile frontier against Indian raids.

From 1759 to the outbreak of the American Revolution, Washington enjoyed a placid life, managing his lands around Mount Vernon and serving in the Virginia House of Burgesses. Married to a widow, Martha Dandridge Custis, he devoted himself to a busy but happy round of life.

Like his fellow planters, Washington felt himself exploited by British merchants and hampered by British Government regulations. His experiences both as a planter and as a military leader made him increasingly dissatisfied with the Crown.

As the quarrel with the mother country grew increasingly acute, Washington moderately but firmly voiced his resistance to British restrictions. He warned, ". . . more blood will be spilt . . . if the ministry are determined to push matters to extremity, than history has ever yet furnished instances of in the annals of North America."

Washington was elected a delegate to the

REBUILT STOCKADE *and storehouse revive Fort Necessity near Union (now Uniontown), Pennsylvania. Washington built the fort in 1754, after leading a surprise attack on a French detachment. The incident touched off the French and Indian War. A month later the French retaliated, throwing a 900-man force against the fort. After a day's fighting in a driving rainstorm, Washington surrendered and returned to Virginia with his disarmed men. The defeat—his only formal surrender—induced Great Britain to send an expedition to Virginia under Gen. Edward Braddock. Washington joined him as an aide.*

WASHINGTON READS *the burial service over General Braddock. Ignorant of frontier warfare, Braddock rejected the idea of fighting French and Indians with their own guerrilla tactics. As he advanced on Fort Duquesne (Pittsburgh) in 1755, he and half his men fell in battle. Retreating wagons ran over Braddock's grave to obliterate all signs lest Indians dig up the body for its scalp.*

LIBRARY OF CONGRESS

Second Continental Congress. By the time it assembled in Philadelphia in May, 1775, the battles at Lexington and Concord had taken place. Now a southerner was needed to command the minutemen assembled at Cambridge. Such a leader would bring the backing of all the colonies to the struggle thus far confined to New England. Of all the delegates to the Continental Congress, Washington was most imposing in his chosen blue uniform as a Virginia militia commander, and Congress elected him commander in chief.

On July 3, 1775, at Cambridge, Massachusetts, Washington assumed command of the ill-trained army and embarked upon a war that was to last six grueling years. The unwillingness of the British to grant concessions soon made apparent to him that this must be a war for independence—a viewpoint Congress confirmed on July 4, 1776.

Washington faced discouraging obstacles. The new state governments were usually lukewarm in their support, and Congress seldom gave him the men and supplies he needed. Washington, far from assuming dictatorial powers, was compliant with the orders of Congress, even, at times, when they went against his military judgment.

Working such long hours that biographers 13

CLYDE HARE © NATIONAL GEOGRAPHIC SOCIETY

FIRST FIRST LADY. *Martha Washington paid $28 to Charles Willson Peale to paint this miniature in 1776 when she was 45. Later she described herself as an "old-fashioned Virginia house-keeper, steady as a clock, busy as a bee, and cheerful as a cricket."*

MOUNT VERNON *yearly receives more than a million visitors, who respond to Washington's own invitation: "I have no objection to any sober or orderly person's gratifying their curiosity in viewing the buildings, Gardens & ca...."*

have wondered when he found time to sleep, he somehow managed to build and maintain an army. He realized early that the best strategy for his weak, inexperienced troops was to harass the British rather than risk an all-out assault. He reported to Congress that "we should on all Occasions avoid a general Action, or put anything to the Risque, unless compelled by a necessity, into which we ought never to be drawn."

In ensuing years, from time to time he fell back slowly before superior British forces, then struck unexpectedly. It was sound strategy, and Washington an able commander.

Above all, he demonstrated his singular

organizing talents and his unparalleled fortitude in the face of adversity. It was this fortitude that carried him through the bleak winter of 1777-78 at Valley Forge, its log huts now restored. It also carried him through later discouragements, even after—with the aid of French allies—he had forced in 1781 the surrender of Lord Cornwallis at Yorktown, where earthworks still bristle with cannon.

Yorktown ended the active fighting, but the Continental Army remained unpaid and restless. To Washington's acute dismay, one of the colonels proposed making him king. But, like his Roman model Cincinnatus, he

MOUNT VERNON LADIES' ASSOCIATION (LEFT) AND THOMAS NEBBIA © N.G.S.

wished upon the conclusion of peace in 1783 to retire to his fields.

BACK at Mount Vernon, Washington came to realize that the American Nation under its Confederation Government was not functioning very well. Powers were inadequate to maintain respect for American shippers, to protect the frontier against incursions by British fur traders and Indians, or to restrain the states from engaging in economic reprisals against each other.

"Internal dissentions, and jarrings with our Neighbours," he wrote, "are not only productive of mischievous consequences, as it respects ourselves, but has a tendency to lessen our national character, and importance in the eyes of European powers."

The news that Massachusetts farmers had taken up arms against heavy taxation led Washington to lament, "We are fast verging to anarchy and confusion!" Hence he became an influential mover in the steps leading to the Constitutional Convention at Philadelphia in the summer of 1787.

Washington, presiding over the Convention, took little part in the debates, but lent his conciliatory talents and his prestige to the framing of a stronger government. When the Constitution was ratified and the new

15

LIBRARY OF CONGRESS (BELOW)

CLOUDS OF CANNON SMOKE *boil above the Princeton battlefield as Washington,*
on horseback with sword extended, directs artillery. Continental victory on
January 3, 1777, climaxed a daring drive that gained for Washington a military
reputation at home and abroad. Ten days earlier, on Christmas night, the general
had ferried his weather-beaten troops across the ice-clogged Delaware (left) and
staged a surprise attack on Trenton, routing the holiday-happy enemy in a two-
hour engagement.

Surging on toward Princeton, the Continentals encountered Trenton-bound
British reinforcements dispatched by Cornwallis to "bag the fox" beside the
now impassable Delaware. In the bleak orchard (above) outside the college town,
Washington's tired forces dealt the enemy a second stinging blow.

Deaf-mute William Mercer painted the action in which his father, American
Brig. Gen. Hugh Mercer, lost his life. The Historical Society of Pennsylvania
owns the primitive work of art.

17

SILVER EAGLE *adorned a cockade on Washington's hat. The accessories below served the Father of his Country through the years of the Revolution. Mount Vernon displays the mementos.*

BONE-INLAID KNIFE *and fork went with the general on his campaigns.*

SILVER SPURS *were given by Washington to Lt. Thomas Lamb during cold and hungry days at Valley Forge.*

IN WHIPPING WINDS AND DRIFTING SNOW, *Washington and young Lafayette share their soldiers' hardships in the bitter winter of 1777-78 at Valley Forge. Only the general's indomitable will held together the Continental Army of 11,000 men.*

MOUNT VERNON LADIES' ASSOCIATION (ABOVE); ENGRAVING BY H. B. HALL FROM CHAPPEL, LIBRARY OF CONGRESS

LORD CORNWALLIS'S *army marches out of Yorktown in surrender on October 19, 1781—decisive battle of the Revolution. Victory marked the end of six years in which Washington had fought the British. Declining salary, he paid his own expenses; Congress reimbursed him after the war.*

In John Trumbull's oil painting, displayed in the U. S. Capitol, Washington sits on a brown charger. His deputy, Maj. Gen. Benjamin Lincoln, on the white horse, conducts the British troops to stack their arms. Washington delegated the honor because Lord Cornwallis refused to appear.

UNITED STATES CAPITOL HISTORICAL SOCIETY © NATIONAL GEOGRAPHIC SOCIETY

machinery of government began to operate, the electoral college unanimously cast its ballots for Washington for President. With considerable misgivings, he accepted.

On April 30, 1789, Washington, standing on the balcony of Federal Hall on Wall Street in New York, took his oath of office as the first President of the United States (page 25). When he entered the Senate Chamber to deliver his Inaugural Address before the assembled Congress, his face was grave, his words almost inaudible.

The challenge facing President Washington and the fledgling Government gave him full reason to be grave. The United States was a weak agricultural republic in a world dominated by large unfriendly monarchies. Its population in 1790 was only 4,000,000, of whom 700,000 were slaves; its treasury was empty; it had no army or navy worthy of the name. The Constitution was no more than a framework, silent on many details.

"As the first of every thing, *in our situa-tion* will serve to establish a Precedent," Washington wrote James Madison, "it is devoutly wished on my part, that these precedents may be fixed on true principles."

"Washington's Presidency was nothing if not painfully constitutional," Clinton Rossiter has written; Washington "did the new republic a mighty service by proving that power can ennoble as well as corrupt. . . ."

Washington was of no disposition to infringe upon the policy-making powers that he felt the Constitution bestowed upon the Congress, and, except for exploring questions of constitutionality, did not question measures it enacted. On the other hand, the determination of foreign policy became preponderantly a Presidential concern.

When Washington, accepting literally the constitutional proviso that he should negotiate treaties with the advice and consent of the Senate, appeared with a list of queries, the Senators, jealous of their prerogatives, refused him instant answers. "This defeats

19

every purpose of my coming here," Washington fumed. Thereafter he negotiated treaties as he judged best and sent them to the Senate to ratify or reject.

Again, while the Senate, according to the Constitution, had to give its consent to Presidential appointees, Washington insisted he could remove them without permission.

As Chief Executive, Washington gave considerable authority to his department heads, and gradually came to depend upon them for advice, at first through written opinions, then as a Cabinet. At these meetings, unlike most of his successors, he ordinarily did not set forth his own opinion, and unless the Cabinet was evenly divided, followed the recommendation of its majority.

This reluctance to wield executive authority singlehandedly has led many later historians to feel that Washington was eclipsed by his subordinates. It is easy to overlook the fact that Washington, while slow and deliberate, was also thorough in his analysis of problems, and that he was more balanced in judgment than his subordinates. There was never any question at the time but that Washington was President, and that national policies had to have his approval. And Thomas Jefferson in 1796 admitted, "One man outweighs them all in influence over the people."

Jefferson spoke from firsthand knowledge, since clearly, during the years when Jefferson served as Secretary of State (and thereafter also), Washington's was the controlling hand in foreign affairs. Even before he became President, he felt strongly that it would be disastrous to become embroiled in the quarrels of the European titans. He wrote in 1788, "I hope the United States of America will be able to keep disengaged from the labyrinth of European politics and Wars.... It should be the policy of United America to administer to their wants,

"G. WASHINGTON" in the map title opposite shows the autograph of the 19-year-old surveyor. Later he added more flourishes but kept the basic signature.

VICTORIOUS AFTER LONG YEARS OF WAR, *Washington resigns command of the Continental Army to resume the life of a Virginia squire, December 23, 1783.*

PAINTING BY EDWIN WHITE, COURTESY STATE HOUSE, ANNAPOLIS, MARYLAND © N.G.S.

TRAVELS OF G. Washington

© N.G.S.

WASHINGTON'S MAJOR BATTLES

1. Fort Necessity — 1754
2. Fort Duquesne — 1755, 1758
3. Siege of Boston — 1775-76
4. Long Island — 1776
5. Harlem Heights — 1776
6. White Plains — 1776
7. Trenton — 1776
8. Princeton — 1777
9. Brandywine — 1777
10. Germantown — 1777
11. Monmouth — 1778
12. Yorktown — 1781

Battleground : ✗

LAKE ONTARIO

LAKE ERIE

NEW YORK

PENNSYLVANIA

VIRGINIA

TENNESSEE

NORTH CAROLINA

SOUTH CAROLINA

GEORGIA

MD.

DELAWARE

NEW JERSEY

VERMONT

NEW HAMPSHIRE

MASSACHUSETTS

CONNECTICUT

R.I.

DISTRICT OF MAINE

ATLANTIC OCEAN

Crown Point
Fort Ticonderoga
Kittery
Portsmouth
Lexington
Cambridge
Concord
Boston
Cape Cod
Worcester
Springfield
Providence
Newport
Albany
Schenectady
Block House
Fort Schuyler (Rome)
Mohawk
Oneida Lake
Cooperstown
Kingston
Stone Ridge
Hartford
New London
New Haven
Fishkill
Newburgh
Haverstraw
Long Island
Coram
New York
Morristown
Princeton
Trenton
Philadelphia
Wilmington
Reading
Valley Forge
Harrisburg
Lancaster
York
Fort Le Boeuf (Waterford)
Fort Machault (Franklin)
Logs Town (Legionville)
Fort Duquesne (Pittsburgh)
Raystown (Bedford)
Warm Springs
Union (Uniontown)
Fort Cumberland
Hagars Town
Frederick Town
Baltimore
Annapolis
Washington
Alexandria
Mount Vernon
Winchester
Culpeper C.H.
Fredericksburg
Ferry Farm
Wakefield
Tappahanock
Augusta C.H. (Staunton)
Hanover C.H.
Richmond
Williamsburg
Yorktown
Norfolk
Suffolk
Petersburg
Big Lick (Roanoke)
Charlotte Court House
Roanoke
Christiansburg
Fort Mayo
Dismal Swamp
Halifax
Tarborough
Greeneville
Newbern
Guilford
Salem
Nuse
Charlottesburg (Charlotte)
Wilmington
Camden
Columbia
Georgetown
Augusta
Charleston
Waynesborough
Savannah
Fort Le Boeuf
Arbuckle

Crossing the Allegheny

Crossing the Delaware

Surveying the Frontier

Touring the South

George Washington's Compass

Potomack

Shenando

Monongahela

Ohio

Allegheny

Susquehanna

Delaware

Hudson

Chesapeake Bay

Delaware Bay

James

York

Santee

Savannah

Great Pedee

NW Cape Fear

To Barbados

1732-1758, Surveying and the French-Indian Campaign
1759-1774, Before the War
1775-1783, Revolutionary War
1784-1799, After the War
★ United States Capitals During George Washington's Lifetime

0 — 100 — 200
Scale of miles

National Geographic Map by Lisa Biganzoli and John Garst after Aaron Arrowsmith's map of 1796 © N.G.S.

SOLDIER TURNED STATESMAN, *Washington (on podium) presides at the Philadelphia Convention on May 25, 1787, despite a vow never again to leave his beloved Mount Vernon. Patriots called the meeting hoping to draw together the divergent states and to build the framework for a new national government. As presiding officer, Washington seldom lent his voice to the debates that raged through the scorching summer months, but his strength became a silent, firm guideline. At times during the proceedings it looked as though the 55 delegates could never reach any sort of meeting ground.*

On one occasion the venerable Benjamin Franklin (seated far left with cane) rose and with tremulous voice moved that they pray: "The small progress we have made after

four or five weeks' close attendance . . . is, methinks, a melancholy proof of the imperfection of human understanding. . . . How has it happened, that we have not hitherto once thought of humbly applying to the Father of Lights to illuminate our understandings?" But still the wrangling grew hotter, and even Washington's faith wavered. He wrote Hamilton in July, *"they are now, if possible, in a worse train than ever; you will find but little ground on which the hope of a good establishment can be formed. In a word, I almost despair of seeing a favourable issue."* But two months later, on September 12, the writing committee entered the chamber with a product molded by argument and tempered by reason—the Constitution of the United States.

23

BY JUNIUS BRUTUS STERNS, FROM VIRGINIA MUSEUM OF FINE ARTS, GIFT OF COLONEL AND MRS. EDGAR W. GARBISCH

without being engaged in their quarrels."

When the French Revolution led to a major war between France and England, Thomas Jefferson, Washington's Secretary of State, was ardently pro-French, and Alexander Hamilton, his Secretary of the Treasury, equally pro-British. Washington insisted upon a middle course. Given twenty years, he believed, the American Nation could become sufficiently powerful to "bid defiance in a just cause to any power whatever." Thanks to Washington, the United States gained those twenty years.

In one respect, Washington failed to envisage the direction the American Commonwealth would take. Like many of his contemporaries, he found political parties repugnant. He expected to be "President of all the people" and was disappointed when two parties began to develop. He tried to keep both contending leaders, Hamilton and Jefferson, within his Cabinet. But his was more nearly the Hamiltonian position. At the end of 1793 Jefferson resigned, and by 1795 Washington was appointing to office only men of known Federalist views.

In creating respect for the United States, Washington felt he must comport himself with as much formality and ceremony as though he were a republican monarch. The firm insistence upon ceremonial had its advantages. When Washington visited Massa-

MASTER OARSMEN *row the Father of his Country up the East River. New York City tumultuously welcomes the hero, arriving for his first Inaugural. Washington recorded himself both pleased and pained by "the display of boats . . . the roar of cannon, and the loud acclamations."*

FIRST IN PEACE, *Washington takes his oath of office as the first President of the infant Republic, April 30, 1789. From now on, his every action will set a precedent. Hand on Bible, he stands on the balcony of a Wall Street building lent by New York City as a Federal Capitol.*

ENGRAVING BY J. ROGERS FROM J. McNEVIN © N.G.S.

LIBRARY OF CONGRESS

chusetts at the end of his first year in office, Governor John Hancock tried to force the President to pay the first call, and, failing, gave way. The President, it became clear, would take precedence over governors.

Wearied of politics, feeling old and tired, Washington determined to retire at the end of his second term. In September, 1796, as his political testament, he published a Farewell Address in which he urged his countrymen to form a union of hearts and minds, foreswearing excessive party spirit and geographical distinctions. In foreign affairs, he warned against long-term alliances. The United States should demonstrate to Europe that "we act for *ourselves,* and not for *others.*"

Washington enjoyed less than three years of retirement at Mount Vernon, for he died of a throat infection December 14, 1799. The four-poster in which he lay still stands in his room looking down on the Potomac.

For months the entire Nation mourned him. Orators and preachers paid flowery tribute, but said less than Abigail, the wife of President John Adams, who commented to her sister: "He never grew giddy, but ever maintained a modest diffidence of his own talents. . . . Possessed of power, possessed of an extensive influence, he never used it but for the benefit of his country. . . . If we look through the whole tenor of his life, history will not produce to us a parallel."

BY EDWARD SAVAGE, NATIONAL GALLERY OF ART, ANDREW MELLON COLLECTION

FREED AT LAST *of public burden, Washington returns to spend his few remaining years as squire of Mount Vernon. A family portrait (left) depicts him with his wife and her grandchildren, George Washington Parke Custis and Eleanor Parke Custis.*

Making the daily rounds of Mount Vernon (right), he appears bent and white-haired. Less than three years after retirement, on December 14, 1799, he died of a throat infection, to remain for all time "first in the hearts of his countrymen."

SIMPLE FAMILY TOMB, *requested by Washington, stands on a site he selected in a pleasantly wooded glen at Mount Vernon. Honoring his wish to lie beside Martha at the plantation, Washington's heirs denied an appeal to move his body to the Capitol.*

MOURNING A DEPARTED LEADER: *Grief-stricken citizens pay homage to a stylized tombstone bearing Washington's likeness in this engraving.*

NEW YORK PUBLIC LIBRARY

The Monument: Tribute in Stone

By LONNELLE AIKMAN

L IKE THE PYRAMIDS of Egypt or the Eiffel Tower in Paris, the Washington National Monument in the American Capital etches against the sky a profile that is known around the world.

"An exclamation point five hundred and fifty-five feet high," a novelist once described this tribute to the soldier-statesman who was first in the hearts of his country-

FLAG AT THE MONUMENT FLIES AT HALF-STAFF AS THE NATION MOURNS THE DEATH OF PRESIDENT JOHN F. KENNEDY; JAMES P. BLAIR © N.G.S.

men. "Mathematics in action," said an architectural historian in pointing out "the purity of its abstract form." And all can see in the starkly soaring obelisk a marble symbol of George Washington's strength and vision.

Rising in a city where great Government buildings grow horizontally instead of vertically, the Washington Monument easily dwarfs everything surrounding it.

Shimmering in the sun by day, a pillar of light by night, it reaches peak display once a year when Fourth of July fireworks trace the familiar silhouette in shooting stars and showers of colored flowers (page 57).

Washington, D. C., is hard to imagine without "the Monument," as everybody knows it. Since its completion in 1884, more than 43 million people have ridden or trudged to the top for a breathtaking view of the Capital. To many a citizen, the sight of this spire stirs nostalgic memories of childhood, when climbing its 898 steps was heroic challenge, and hopping and skipping down again sheer physical delight.

Yet the creation of a fitting memorial to George Washington in the city that bears his name—and whose site he personally selected—was no small task. Indeed, the project took a full century to come to fruition, and faced so many problems that at times its supporters were all but forced to abandon it entirely.

The idea first bloomed in the earliest days of the Republic, amid widespread rejoicing over the victorious Revolution.

In August, 1783, the Continental Congress, then meeting in Princeton, resolved "(Unanimously, ten States being present) That an equestrian statue of General Washington be erected at the place where the

B. ANTHONY STEWART © N.G.S.

HALF-CLAD HERO *of marble once occupied the Capitol Rotunda and later the Capitol grounds. Public disapproval caused its removal, in 1908, to the Smithsonian Institution.*

residence of Congress shall be established."

The general was highly gratified by the action, as he wrote a former comrade in arms. Such flattering testimonials of regard from his country were, "and I trust ever will be," he observed, "the most pleasing reflection of my life."

Later, after Congress had voted to build the new seat of Government by the Potomac, President Washington approved the spot assigned his statue by city planner L'Enfant. It should stand on the Mall, they agreed, at an intersection of lines west and south of the future Capitol and President's House.

But the fledgling Nation had more pressing problems, and Washington himself felt that the low state of the treasury scarcely warranted such nonessential expenses.

So it was not until his death in 1799 that Americans suddenly realized that they had failed to provide a monument in appreciation of the Father of their Country. As hundreds of impassioned eulogies rang out from pulpit and podium across the land, Congress passed another resolution.

The new bill was sponsored by Representative John Marshall, destined to become the pioneering Chief Justice who would establish the power of the Supreme Court.

Marshall's proposal called for a marble memorial inside the Capitol building, to which Washington's remains were to be transferred when, and if, permission could be obtained from the family. Reluctantly Martha Washington agreed.

Eventually, after decades of Congressional debates, resolutions, and correspondence with Washington's heirs, a mausoleum was provided under the Capitol's Rotunda. Congress even proposed, as Washington's birthday centennial approached in 1832, that the bodies of both George and Martha should rest there.

But the tomb was never occupied. Washington's grandnephew and current Mount Vernon owner, John Augustine Washington, refused to allow the remains to be moved, citing the general's will that had directed his burial on the Virginia estate.

Henceforth the Capitol tomb would remain a tourist curiosity, and in time the repository for the black-draped catafalque on which have rested the bodies of all Presi-

Richmond Nov.ʳ 25.ᵗʰ 1833

Dear Sir

I received yesterday your letter of the 22.ᵈ informing me that the Washington monumental society has done me the honor to chuse me as its president. You are right in supposing that the most ardent wish of my heart is to see some lasting testimonial of the grateful affection of his country erected to the memory of her first citizen; I have always wished it, and have always thought that the metropolis of the union was the fit place for this national monument. I cannot therefore refuse to take any place which the society may assign me; and though my advanced age forbids the hope of being useful, I am encouraged by the name of the first vice President to believe that in him ample compensation will be found for any defects in the President.

With great respect and esteem I am dear Sir your obedt

J Marshall

SUPREME COURT OF THE UNITED STATES (LEFT), NATIONAL ARCHIVES (ABOVE), AND RARE BOOKS, LIBRARY OF CONGRESS

MEN OF ACTION: *Chief Justice John Marshall (left) and former Librarian of Congress George Watterston in 1833 organized a movement which led to the formation of the Washington National Monument Society.*

dents, beginning with Lincoln, who have lain in state in the Rotunda above.

The Congress of the 1830's was still bent, however, on honoring Washington at the legislative heart of the Nation. In July, 1832, it authorized the then huge sum of $5,000 for a marble statue to be executed by "a suitable artist" and displayed in the Rotunda. Horatio Greenough, an American sculptor working in Italy, won the commission.

As it turned out, Greenough's classical concept of Washington, which took the form of a 20-ton seated figure, bare-chested and loosely draped, proved almost as big a fiasco as the vacant tomb (page 30).

The public was shocked when the statue was unveiled about 1841. The dignified general appeared, it was said, as if "entering or leaving a bath." Shortly after, the figure was deemed inappropriate for the Rotunda floor. It was removed to the grounds and suffered the whims of the weather until Congress finally transferred it to the exhibit halls of the Smithsonian Institution.

Meantime, a civic movement was getting under way in Washington to build the towering obelisk we see today.

The project began modestly in 1833 with a paragraph in the September 24 issue of the Capital newspaper *National Intelligencer*. It announced a meeting at City Hall of "Those gentlemen who have expressed their desire" to join a group planning a monument to George Washington's memory.

Behind the new organization, which called itself the Washington National Monument Society, stood some of the town's leading citizens. Guiding spirit was the former Librarian of Congress, George Watterston, an energetic gentleman of Scottish descent who also practiced law and politics, edited newspapers, wrote novels, guidebooks, and poetry—and fathered eight children.

George Washington's old friend, John Marshall, now 78 and full of honors, was elected the society's first president. After Marshall, the post went to former United States President James Madison, and later —ex officio—to each successive President, from Andrew Jackson to Lyndon Johnson.

Not only was the monument project linked from the beginning with the Nation's leaders, but during the next half century,

WINNING ENTRY: *The design of Robert Mills, onetime draftsman for Thomas Jefferson and eminent architect of the day, captured first place in the Monument Society's 1836 competition for a Washington memorial that would "harmoniously blend durability, simplicity, and grandeur."*

Mills had already won acclaim with his memorial to Washington commissioned by the City of Baltimore, Maryland, and completed in 1829. Appointed U.S. architect by President Jackson in 1836, he designed many public buildings, among them the U.S. Treasury, the Patent Office, and the General Post Office.

Mills's plan for the Washington Monument for the District of Columbia (opposite), as he described it, outlined a "grand circular colonnaded building ... 100 feet high, from which springs an obelisk shaft ... making a total elevation of 600 feet."

The columned base, its frieze studded with seals of all the states, held statues of Revolutionary leaders and frescoes and paintings of battle scenes. Its entrance served as a pedestal for a classical Washington driving a triumphal chariot.

The Monument Society never accepted the ornate base, concentrating instead on raising money to construct the obelisk. Mills estimated $1,250,000 as the cost of executing his design. But the figure was conservative; today's unadorned shaft cost $1,187,710.

LIBRARY OF CONGRESS (ABOVE LEFT) AND KIPLINGER COLLECTION

its building progress alternately zoomed and lagged with ups and downs in the fortunes of the country at large.

Andrew Jackson began his second term the same year the Monument Society was founded. But even as his joyful followers celebrated the triumph of the "People's President," a bitter political war over finance was brewing between Jackson, Con-

gress, and the Government-chartered Bank of the United States, a power in its own right.

With the national economy shaken by this dispute concerning the Bank's policies, it hardly seemed an auspicious time to seek funds for an ambitious patriotic memorial.

Nevertheless, the society launched its first drive, sending notices to leading newspapers, appealing to individuals, church,

business, and civic groups. All ranks of Americans were asked to contribute, with an initial limit of $1 a person.

By 1836 some $28,000 had been collected, then invested by "gentlemen of prudence and elevated moral worth," as an announcement assured contributors. True, this sum was a drop in the bucket compared to the estimated million-dollar cost. But it

ROBERT C. MAGIS, NATIONAL GEOGRAPHIC STAFF © N.G.S.

"WINE OF JOY" *consecrates the Monument's cornerstone as Grand Master Benjamin French leads Masonic rites of dedication on July 4, 1848. President James K. Polk and Dolley Madison (above parasol) witness the proceedings from a nearby stand. The stone, containing many tokens of the time, was laid at the northeast corner of the foundation.*

offered sufficient promise to launch a public invitation to American architects to submit competing designs for the structure.

Contest winner was the well-known architect-engineer Robert Mills (page 32), who already had designed a smaller Washington Monument in Baltimore, and soon would be creating the Treasury, Patent Office, and Post Office buildings in the Capital City.

Mills's entry fitted 19th-century taste in neoclassic art to a curlicued "T." It provided for a 600-foot obelisk, surrounded at the base by a circular, colonnaded Greek temple 100 feet high. Behind the columns, 30 niches stood ready to receive statues of prominent Americans. Above the central portico, a colossal toga-clad Washington drove a battle chariot drawn by Arabian steeds (page 33).

All this had to be discarded later, when the required funds—perhaps fortunately— were lacking. Only the obelisk remained. And it was 1848 before construction began, following the Government's donation of public land near the site originally selected for Washington's equestrian statue.

"... Few left the city, while great multi-

MATHEW BRADY, LIBRARY OF CONGRESS

THE MEMORY
—OF—
GEORGE WASHINGTON.
EVERY true lover of his country will contribute something this day, in aid of the

Great National Monument
—TO—
WASHINGTON!

Have ready your donation, however small. The Contribution Box and the Ballot Box are this day side by side at every Poll in the United States.

The County in this State making the largest contribution in proportion to the number of votes cast, will be presented with an elegant three-quarter size MARBLE STATUE OF WASHINGTON, valued at $500.

CALIFORNIA, Nov. 6, 1860.

☞ Please put up this notice in the immediate vicinity of the Polls on election day, so that every voter can be ready with his contribution.

UNSIGHTLY STUMP *stood for two decades as a mute reminder of the Nation's neglect. Political turmoil and dwindling funds halted construction in 1854.*

APPEAL FOR FUNDS: *Broadsides posted at polling places across the land remind voters in 1860 of their obligation to their first President. This election brought Lincoln to the White House.*

CATTLE PEN *in the Civil War: Monument grounds serve Union forces as a stockyard and slaughterhouse in this contemporary print.*

NATIONAL ARCHIVES (ABOVE) AND LIBRARY OF CONGRESS

tudes rushed into it. . . . The weather was most propitious. . . . The spectacle was beautiful to behold." So reported the *National Intelligencer* after the cornerstone laying, July 4, 1848, at the Monument grounds.

Gathered on the knoll's broad slopes were 15 to 20 thousand people, including the military in dress uniforms, fraternal groups, Indian delegations, and the Federal Government's great and near-great (pages 34-5).

President Polk attended, "though in feeble health," as he wrote in his diary. So did a little-known Congressman named Abraham Lincoln, together with two other future Presidents, Buchanan and Johnson.

Present also were Martha Washington's grandson, George Washington Parke Custis; Mrs. Alexander Hamilton, still active at 91; and Mrs. James (the incomparable Dolley) Madison. Nor did commentators fail to mention another notable participant—a live American eagle chained to a draped arch for symbolic atmosphere. This very bird had greeted Lafayette 24 years before, when nearby Alexandria welcomed the general on his return to the country he had helped free.

The Speaker of the House of Representatives, Robert C. Winthrop, gave the main address of the Monument inaugural, an hour-and-a-half oration on "The Character of Washington." In laying the cornerstone, the Grand Master of the city's Masonic

NATIONAL PARK SERVICE

POTOMAC MARSHES OF 1875 *covered future sites of the Lincoln Memorial and the Reflecting Pool. On reclaimed land four decades later, work started on the Greek temple honoring Lincoln. A new, broad Constitution Avenue supplanted B Street (right) in 1931. In this view from the Smithsonian Institution, gardens of the Department of Agriculture pattern the Mall; abandoned Monument rises like a factory smokestack.*

hours in broiling heat. Returning to the White House afterward, he became ill. In five days he was dead of what the doctors diagnosed as cholera morbus; legend says his death resulted from eating quantities of iced milk and cherries.

FOR THE FIRST FEW YEARS the Monument grew like a marble beanstalk. To speed the process, the society had invited all the states and territories, patriotic citizens, and even friendly foreign countries to contribute stone blocks to embellish the interior walls. Among the first presented were stones from Maine, Delaware, and the Franklin Fire Company of Washington, D. C. Some went into place at the 30-foot landing as early as 1849.

From inscriptions carved on many of the 190 memorials that greet walkers at 10-foot intervals, you sense now the pride of a growing Nation. Kansas and Wyoming were territories when they sent offerings. On a block cut in 1852 California called herself the "Youngest Sister of the Union."

As sectional tension deepened before the Civil War, the word "Union" marked many a stone. "KNOWS NO NORTH, NO SOUTH. NOTHING BUT THE UNION," Indiana proclaimed proudly.

When you climb from landing to landing today, you come on blocks from such donors as the Cherokee Nation, the Sons of Temperance, and the "Ladies & Gentlemen of the Dramatic Profession of America."

Greece, "The Mother of Ancient Liberty," sent a white marble piece from the ruins of the Parthenon. Turkey's sultan inscribed his gift with sentiments composed by his court poet. A "Company of [Chinese] *(Continued on page 44)*

Lodge used the same silver trowel held by Washington at the Capitol's stone-setting ritual of 1793.

That night, as fireworks sparkled and sputtered in honor of the occasion, the spectators had more to celebrate than they knew. For President Polk at the Executive Mansion was preparing a proclamation to announce some news. It would tell the Nation that Mexico had ratified the treaty ending the Mexican War and adding half a million square miles to the American West.

Less pleasant to recall is another Fourth of July celebration that took place at the Monument grounds two years later. On this occasion, President Zachary Taylor sat for

(Continued on page 44)

MIGHT-HAVE-BEEN MONUMENTS, *designed on the eve of the 100th anniversary of American Independence, reflected growing concern over the unsightly pile of stones that had marred the Mall for so long. Would-be designers, both professional and self-appointed, suggested various fates for the project.*

Some advocated tearing down the partially finished structure and beginning anew; others favored completing it to the height originally planned, but with variations; still others offered plans that would merely adorn the portion of the shaft already standing.

An anonymous Californian submitted to the American Architect *an interesting solution (opposite). A contemporary critic described the "spirited and*

poetic composition" as reflecting the "modern French Renaissance," and having "affinity with some of the better Hindu pagodas." At the temple's footing, a Washington of massive proportions sat enthroned, with mounted guards at his sides and several feminine figures draped at his feet.

In August, 1876, after the Monument Society had abandoned hope of raising funds to complete the memorial, it asked the Federal Government for help. Authorities settled on a simple obelisk of true Egyptian proportions after consulting with U.S. Minister to Italy George P. Marsh, an authority on architecture. The U.S. Army Corps of Engineers began work in 1878.

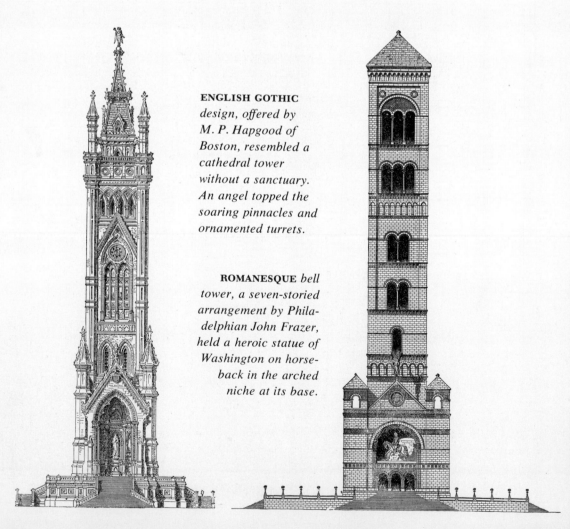

ENGLISH GOTHIC *design, offered by M. P. Hapgood of Boston, resembled a cathedral tower without a sanctuary. An angel topped the soaring pinnacles and ornamented turrets.*

ROMANESQUE *bell tower, a seven-storied arrangement by Phila- delphian John Frazer, held a heroic statue of Washington on horse- back in the arched niche at its base.*

LIBRARY OF CONGRESS

DYNAMIC ENGINEER *Lt. Col. Thomas L. Casey, builder of Civil War forts, took charge of the Monument in 1878 and saw the project through.*

WORK STARTS ANEW: *Engineers excavate for new underpinning after finding that the original rubble masonry base would be inadequate to support the structure's completed weight. Digging out 70 percent of the ground under the shaft, they poured a deep concrete slab below the old foundation. They then strengthened and balanced the whole by enclosing it in a concrete skirt. Broadened base (below) awaits final reinforcement before upward growth.*

HARPER'S WEEKLY (ABOVE) AND LIBRARY OF CONGRESS

GROWTH OF THE MONUMENT

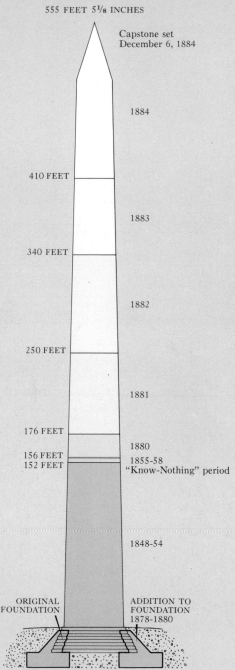

555 FEET 5⅛ INCHES

Capstone set
December 6, 1884

1884

410 FEET

1883

340 FEET

1882

250 FEET

1881

176 FEET

156 FEET — 1880
152 FEET — 1855-58
"Know-Nothing" period

1848-54

ORIGINAL
FOUNDATION

ADDITION TO
FOUNDATION
1878-1880

Cornerstone laid July 4, 1848

WORK PROCEEDED *smoothly on the first 152 feet of the Monument. But in 1854, construction virtually ceased for a quarter century. In 1878, U. S. Army Engineers removed four feet of inferior masonry laid by the "Know-Nothings." Thereafter, the shaft grew on an average of 80 feet annually until completion.*

Christians" presented another, covered with Oriental characters and asking ". . . can any man, in ancient or modern times, fail to pronounce Washington peerless?"

But the most famous stone in Monument history—a marble slab from the Temple of Concord in Rome—never reached its place. The gift of Pope Pius IX, it was stolen from the grounds near dawn on March 6, 1854, when the obelisk had risen 152 feet.

"A Deed of Barbarism,"a local newspaper called it, in reporting how a band of masked hoodlums had overpowered the night watchman and rolled the stone in a handcart to the river's edge. There, it was assumed, the thieves either broke up their prize, or rowed out into the Potomac and dumped it.

The block was never recovered, nor was anyone arrested for the crime. It was common belief, however, later substantiated by confessed participants, that the vandals were members of the "Know-Nothing" Party—a political group then campaigning against all Roman Catholics and foreigners.

Furthermore, the following year a gang of Washington Know-Nothings seized control of the Monument Society by an illegal election. The usurpers voluntarily returned the project to its legitimate leaders after several years, having added a few feet of inferior stonework that had to be removed.

But now the Civil War loomed. All work on the Monument ceased, despite the society's redoubled efforts to raise money by placing collection boxes in post offices and at voting polls—including those for the national election that brought Abraham Lincoln to the Presidency.

All during the war, the Monument stump stood as a reminder of the break between the states. Soldiers in blue drilled under the

COMPLETE AT LAST! *Engineers slide the 3,300-pound capstone into place on the obelisk's tip, December 6, 1884. Members of the Washington Monument Society huddle on the lower platform built 500 feet up. Reporters and invited guests climb the frail outside ladder for a closer look under an American flag drawn erroneously by a contemporary artist. Newspapers hailed the Monument's completion, accomplished without a single loss of life.*

COLUMBIA HISTORICAL SOCIETY

Alex Miller del.

WHITE HOUSE COLLECTION (BELOW) AND LIBRARY OF CONGRESS

DEDICATION DAY: *Crowds braved snow and winds that "seemed to come from every point of the compass" to witness the ceremony on February 21, 1885. Many spectators took refuge from the cold in the pavilion erected for the occasion at the Monument's base. Others watched from carriages.*

Pioneer photographer Mathew Brady took this picture of Lt. Gen. Philip H. Sheridan's troops lined up for review by President Chester A. Arthur (above).

Shortly afterward, the Chief Executive doffed his silk hat and put aside his heavy gloves. "... I do now," he said, "... in behalf of the people, receive this Monument ... and declare it dedicated from this time forth to the immortal name and memory of George Washington."

The procession moved on to the Capitol to hear an address prepared by Robert Winthrop, principal speaker at the 1848 cornerstone ceremony.

The newly laid-out Ellipse, a park south of the White House, spreads beyond B Street, today's Constitution Avenue.

46

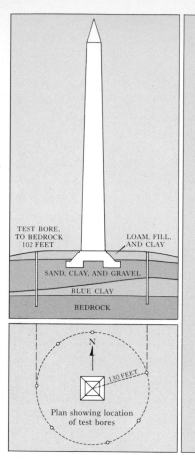

TEST BORE, TO BEDROCK 102 FEET

LOAM, FILL, AND CLAY

SAND, CLAY, AND GRAVEL

BLUE CLAY

BEDROCK

N

130 FEET

Plan showing location of test bores

MONUMENT AT A GLANCE

Cornerstone laid	July 4, 1848
Dedicated	February 21, 1885
Opened to public	October 9, 1888
Total cost	$1,187,710
Material used on face of shaft	White marble*
Height from floor	555 feet 5$\frac{1}{8}$ inches
Width at base	55 feet 1$\frac{1}{2}$ inches
Width at top of shaft	34 feet 5$\frac{1}{2}$ inches
Thickness of walls at base	15 feet
Thickness of walls at top of shaft	18 inches
Weight of monument	81,120 tons
Weight of foundation	36,912 tons
Depth of foundation	36 feet 10 inches
Area of foundation	16,002 square feet
Memorial stones	190
Present elevator installed	1959
Elevator ascent	60 seconds
Exterior cleaned and pointed	1934 and 1964

*From Maryland and Massachusetts

SPONGY SOIL *of sand and clay prevented deep terracing of Monument grounds first proposed in 1901. Lt. Col. Ulysses S. Grant 3rd directed test borings in 1930 that proved the alterations would have undermined the foundation, producing a "Leaning Tower of Washington."*

United States flag that floated over its flat top. Cattle grazed at the depot set up on the grounds to help feed the Army (page 37). Across the way, workmen raised the Capitol's new iron dome—a sign that the Union would go on, as Lincoln had said.

In the war's last April days, the Monument stub saw the Capitol's completed dome spangled with gas lights celebrating the fall of Richmond, then draped in black mourning for the assassinated President whose body lay in the Rotunda below.

The shaft was still untouched when Mark Twain worked as a Washington newspaperman in 1867. "It has the aspect," he wrote later, "of a factory chimney with the top broken off. . . . Cow-sheds about its base . . . contented sheep nibbling pebbles in the desert solitudes . . . tired pigs dozing in the holy calm of its protecting shadow."

By the centennial of Independence in 1876, the sorry state of Washington's memorial had needled the conscience of Capital officials. Congress passed a law, signed by President Grant, providing for Government completion and maintenance of the Monument. At the same time, the Monument Society ceded the land and shaft to the United States, while Congress in turn voted to make the organization a semiofficial advisory body—a status maintained to this day.

Army Engineers on the job soon discovered, however, that the Monument's foundation could not support its proposed height. Before building further, they removed weak sections of the original masonry foundation, and strengthened, broadened, and deepened the rest by filling subterranean tunnels with poured concrete (pages 42-3). So skillful was the substitution that the en-

SKATERS GLEAN the last rosy minutes from a rare day when thick ice covers the Reflecting Pool. In summer children race model sailboats across the shallow panel of water. Unsightly World War II temporary buildings were torn down in 1964 after requests by the Washington National Monument Society.

THOMAS NEBBIA © N.G.S.

KEN HEINEN © N.G.S.

HIGH-PRESSURE JET *of cold water puts final polish on the Monument's exterior walls. This steeplejack performs his duties from the "sky climber," a work basket reserved for the area above platform range.*

SPIDERLIKE MASONS *on steel threads cling to the Monument, risking updrafts that set their walkway swinging. Work in 1964 included repointing corroded mortar seams, replacing cornerstones, and cleaning with sand, brushes, and water. Eight electric platforms replaced scaffolding used for the 1934 cleaning. For this unusual Fisheye-lens shot,* NATIONAL GEOGRAPHIC *photographer Bruce Dale leaned from the upper platform with camera on a 4-foot pole.*

FLASHES OF FIRE *seem to ignite the Monument as lightning splits the skies above Washington. Frozen in bronze on the Virginia side of the Potomac River, United States Marines strain to plant Old Glory atop Mount Suribachi on Iwo Jima.*

THOMAS NEBBIA (LEFT) © N.G.S.; A. C. CHINN, WASHINGTON EVENING STAR

SKY-HIGH WORKMAN *checks lightning rods at the Monument's apex. In the first base-to-tip scrubbing, completed in 1935, a fearless thief scaled the scaffolding and made off with a set of the platinum-tipped conductors.*

tire structure settled only about two inches.

The memorial's dimensions also were changed as a result of research by the U. S. Minister to Italy, George Marsh. A true obelisk, he reported, should have a height about ten times its base width: Hence the Monument's final summit of 555 feet, 5⅛ inches, to a base 55 feet, 1½ inches square.

Finally came the push to the top, starting with a second cornerstone laid by President Hayes in 1880, and ending with the capstone set in place on December 6, 1884.

"... A perfect gale was blowing," said the Washington *Evening Star* in describing the ceremony—held on an open platform built outside the windows 550 feet up (page 45). Officiating was Col. Thomas L. Casey, who had headed planning and construction since the Federal Government took over. As he directed the placing of a solid aluminum tip at the Monument's apex, "a shout went up," wrote the *Star*'s reporter, "the stars and

CHERRY BLOSSOM *princesses and their escorts await the moment of the annual festival coronation. Agriculture Secretary Orville Freeman (left) and television's Mark Evans crown the 1965 queen, Linda Gail Quase.*

Americans have often met in the shadow of the Monument. Drawn by the impartial and just image of the man it symbolizes, they gather here to honor heroes, celebrate victories, and protest injustices.

ED HUFFMAN (LEFT) AND EMORY KRISTOF © N.G.S.

stripes were unfurled and a salute was fired.''

The aluminum tip itself was news. Weighing 100 ounces, at $1.10 an ounce, it was the largest such piece yet cast, and so unusual at the time that it had been displayed in Tiffany's New York jewelry store.

One more ritual and one more President completed the building saga in 1885.

The Monument's dedication began in a pavilion at the grounds on a cold February 21, Washington's birthday falling on Sunday (pages 46-7). President Arthur, bundled in a fur-lined overcoat, his sideburns brushed to stylish points, spoke briefly, then joined the festive parade to warmer quarters in the Capitol's House of Representatives.

The day's main speech was composed by the venerable Robert Winthrop, who had delivered the cornerstone address 37 years before, but who was now too ill to take part. So his Massachusetts colleague, Representative John D. Long, read it for him.

"Our matchless obelisk stands proudly before us today," Winthrop had written in his long, eloquent oration. "The storms of winter must blow and beat upon it. . . . The lightnings of Heaven may scar and blacken it. An earthquake may shake its foundations. . . . But the character which it commemorates and illustrates is secure. . . ."

Yet for all the rejoicing, it was 1888 before the public could climb the stairs or ride the slow steam hoist and peer through the observation room's eight windows.

Indeed, the Washington Monument is never quite finished. An electric elevator replaced the steam lift in 1901, then gave way to improved models in 1926 and 1959. Today's elevator reaches the top in one minute; on the way a recorded voice briefs riders on the story of the memorial.

The lighting system, too, has kept pace with American technological advance. Early visitors found the interior lighted by new—and frightening—electricity, powered by dynamo. You can still see notches in the walls from which the lamps hung, casting flickering beams through the gloom.

While the Monument was still young, an ambitious program to beautify its grounds was proposed, but fortunately not carried out. In 1901, the Senate's McMillan Commission for civic development recommended a landscaping project in line with L'Enfant's original plan for a grandly scenic Mall. The Monument area was to be cut into a series of terraced gardens, embellished with trees, fountains, and a great circular pool.

Since large-scale shifting of earth loads was involved, engineers made deep borings to test subsoil conditions. They found that the Monument itself would be endangered by the excavations, and the proposal was eventually abandoned.

AIR-AGE PERILS brought the obelisk's first exterior searchlights in 1929, outlining its lofty peak. Later the red eyes of aircraft-warning signals began flashing from observation windows, and, in 1958, from holes cut just above for better visibility.

Many other innovations marked the 1958-59 program. In the basement, a giant dehumidifier finally ended an old Monument phenomenon—the moisture condensation that had long precipitated indoor rain.

New floodlights of more than 92-million candlepower were installed. Enveloping the shaft, they created a sword of light, like King Arthur's Excalibur, that pierces the black vault of the Capital's night skies.

Twice a year the Monument's interior is housecleaned. And twice in its lifetime (1934 and 1964) the great marble shell has been repaired and scrubbed from base to tip.

To build and remove the surrounding scaffolding in 1934-35 took three months, longer than the renovation itself. Critics of President Franklin Roosevelt quipped that "That Man in the White House" was crating up the Monument to ship it to Hyde Park.

The latest refurbishing needed only eight platforms. Strung from the top by cables powered by electric winches, they carried workmen up and down the shaft's face, patching, cleaning, and waterproofing. To reach the windswept tip, men rode the sloping surface in individual steel-barred hoists called "sky climbers."

All during the ingenious cleanup, visitors continued to arrive at George Washington's Monument and look out on his forever changing city. Nearly two million came last year, including more and more climbers.

Twenty years ago, only one person in five took to the stairs. Now the ratio is one in three. A 65-year-old man from Kentucky recently walked five round trips while a news reporter kept score below.

The National Park Service, which administers the Monument, has its troubles with pranksters and publicity seekers. Several have tried to walk the stairs on their hands.

Until safety glass covered the openings in 1961, thoughtless people tossed out of the 504-foot-high windows anything from fruit and pennies to rifle shells and skates. A high school football team once managed to hang out its banner, and later a Polish refugee was stopped from unfurling a black shroud protesting world Communism.

One of the few authorized stunts made headlines in January, 1885, even before the Monument's dedication, when a popular baseball star caught a ball dropped from the top. And just before the glass installations, a falling telescopic lens almost killed a guard. Barely missing his head, it broke a woman visitor's wrist.

The Monument has seen five suicides. Before 1926, when window bars were first installed, three men leaped out to their

CRACKLING ROSETTES *spangle the night during the annual Fourth of July fireworks, set off by the National Park Service from the Monument grounds. The obelisk, reflecting the light of 92-million candlepower, glows throughout the year.*

DONALD J. CRUMP © NATIONAL GEOGRAPHIC SOCIETY

PLUSH PADDING *makes early visitors comfortable on the "precarious" 12-minute ride to the top by steam hoist. The first electric lift, installed in 1901, cut time to five minutes. Today's elevator (below), complete with recorded message about the Monument from the National Park Service, offers standing room only for the one-minute ascent.*

LIBRARY OF CONGRESS (ABOVE) AND EMORY KRISTOF © N.G.S.

death. In 1915, and again in 1949, a woman and a man jumped down the elevator shaft.

Misery, however, is a rare visitor at this spot. The Monument—surrounded by its broad, grassy knoll—serves rather as a place of perpetual celebration and recreation.

Here, on Washington's birthday each year, various patriotic groups, including the faithful Monument Society, lay wreaths and make speeches in memory of the man who was "first in war, first in peace."

Tens of thousands of spectators gather here every Fourth of July, to watch the fireworks and share in the national remembrance of that hard-won freedom of long ago.

Under open skies at the Sylvan Theatre, summer audiences fill temporary chairs and spill out over the grounds to watch Shakespearean programs, Cherry Blossom Festivals, popular plays, and musicals.

Fittingly, on Citizenship Day in September, new Americans take the oath of allegiance and salute the 50 flags, one for each state, that ring this memorial. Here, too, come political speakers on controversial subjects, and mass demonstrations like the Prayers-for-Peace Crusade in 1961, and the Civil Rights March, 200,000 strong, in 1963.

During its 80-year span, the great white obelisk has witnessed many an event that mirrored the Nation's current concerns.

One such occurred in the spring of 1887, when National Guard forces from 31 states converged on the Capital to compete in drills of skill and discipline.

"A thousand tents whiten the green sward that stretches around the Washington Monument," the *Evening Star* announced. "Such a camp has not been seen in this country since the veterans of the civil war broke their last camp in '65. Now the soldiers of the North, the South, the East and the West assemble . . . and contend in friendly strife."

Eleven years later, Spanish-American War troops stopped to rest in this same parklike space on their way south to do battle in Cuba. And again in World Wars I and II the green slopes offered a natural assembly and parade ground that sprang to life with martial bands and marching men.

Of all the shows staged with the Monument as backdrop, the largest and liveliest was a bond rally held July 4, 1945, between

EMORY KRISTOF © N.G.S.

VISITORS CRANE *for a look at their lofty destination as they await the elevator. Others (right) walk up the 898 steps to the top, pausing to view the memorial stones. In 1948 fewer than 10 percent of the Monument's visitors walked up; by 1964, the number had increased to 31.4 percent.*

victories in Europe and Asia. An estimated 350,000 people jammed the area for blocks around to see the Cavalcade of Freedom ending the "Mighty Seventh" war loan.

Performers included jeeploads of movie and stage stars, color guards and bands of the Navy, Marines, and Army Air Forces, dozens of patriotic orders, and high-ranking civic, church, and Federal officials.

The acts ranged from songs, dancing, fun, and fireworks to an epic drama of the war and a reading of the Declaration of Independence. Seats bought for the Cavalcade purchased more than $1,250,000 in E bonds.

Through good times and bad, the Wash-

59

ington Monument has stood deep-rooted in American soil and ideals.

Every President since Chester Arthur has looked from the Executive Mansion toward this symbol of responsibility towering at his back door. Grover Cleveland—harried by political and personal slander—spoke of gaining courage in its serene presence.

"From the room where I conduct my high office I hourly see the Monument," said President Hoover in addressing a Joint Session of Congress on the 200th anniversary of Washington's birth. "This shaft is a thing of the spirit. . . . There is about it a mantle of pure radiance. . . ."

On early morning walks, President Truman sometimes strolled to the base of the obelisk and chatted with guards about its history. In 1946, Mr. Truman became the only Chief Executive to go to the top while in office. Together with Secretary of the Interior Harold Ickes and the Monument Society's Ulysses S. Grant 3rd, he obtained from the high windows a perfect view of the proposed site for a new Potomac bridge and of the traffic rerouting needed to reach it.

The Monument's surroundings have vastly improved since 1900, when the Mall area was an unsightly clutter of railroad tracks, haphazard buildings, and marshes.

Massive Government departments, with the Smithsonian Institution's complex of buildings and the National Gallery of Art, now enclose a broad, grassy swath—and still

60

GEORGE F. MOBLEY (BELOW) AND EMORY KRISTOF © N.G.S.

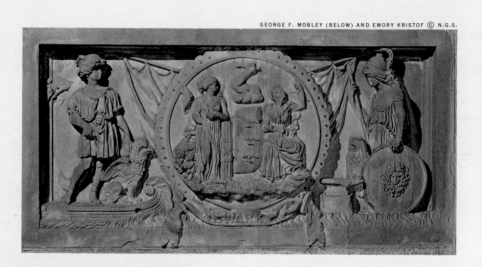

GIFTS OF STONE: *190 memorial blocks from around the world, like these from Newark, N.J., Vermont, and Brazil, brighten granite walls of the stairway. Other stones came from patriotic individuals and groups.*

more green and flowering vistas are planned under the landscape and planting program initiated by President and Mrs. Johnson. The Lincoln and Jefferson Memorials, dedicated in 1922 and 1943 respectively, have added grace and meaning to nearby waterside scenes.

No Capital backdrop, however, is more dramatic than that of the starkly rising Monument and the softly rounded Jefferson Memorial glimpsed through the trees from the south lawn of the White House.

President Johnson, like President Kennedy before him, has made increasing use of this symbolic setting to greet distinguished foreign visitors and to put on official functions, from ballet and fireworks spectacles to lantern-lighted state dinners. Certainly, few could miss the significance of these memorials to the Father of his Country and to democracy's great advocate.

At a press conference held back in the 1920's, a reporter asked President Coolidge what he thought of the then popular vogue for debunking George Washington. Mr. Coolidge turned and gazed out his office window toward the Mall. "I see," he said dryly, "that his Monument's still there."

And so is a still greater testimonial to the man's genius. As Robert Winthrop said in his speech when the Monument was completed at long last, "The Union is itself the all-sufficient and the only sufficient monument to Washington."

61

MARBLE MOSAIC *of horse and palm, salvaged from the ancient African capital of Carthage, recalls the glory of a past civilization.*

Greece's contribution originally formed part of the Parthenon at Athens; another stone is "From the Alexandria Library in Egypt." Still others represent Siam, "Friendly Bremen," Turkey, and Wales.

Donations from foreign nations indicate a far-reaching respect for the character and achievements of America's hero.

HAND PUMPER *of 1854 at the Monument's 250-foot level reflects the pride of the Philadelphia Fire Department. The Monument Society received many stones from civic and trade groups eager to share in the Monument's building. Some of the blocks went into place as early as 1849. Five years later a stone from Pope Pius IX was stolen and never recovered.*

EMORY KRISTOF © N.G.S.

CAPITAL SKYLINE *unfolds beyond the Monument. Almost two million visitors annually see this and three other Washington panoramas from the fiftieth landing.*

EAST *United States Capitol rises on its hill at the end of the Mall, L'Enfant's "Grand Avenue."*

Framing the proud historic dome are Senate Office Buildings (left), Supreme Court, Library of Congress, and House Office Buildings (right).

The white-domed National Gallery of Art gleams left of the 400-foot-wide swath of green which reaches from the Capitol to the Monument grounds.

Six other buildings of the Smithsonian Institution, which sprang from the legacy of James Smithson, an Englishman who never crossed the Atlantic, also flank the Mall. At left rise the Museum of Natural History (center) and, out of view in foreground, the new Museum of History and Technology. At right, towers of the original headquarters rise in red sandstone like a child's sand castle. Behind it cluster the Arts and Industries Building and, unseen, the National Air Museum and Freer Gallery of Art. A new Air and Space Museum will soon occupy the site now filled by flat-roofed temporary office buildings.

Sometimes called "the Nation's attic," the Smithsonian, founded in 1846, is among the world's largest museum complexes and one of America's most popular show places.

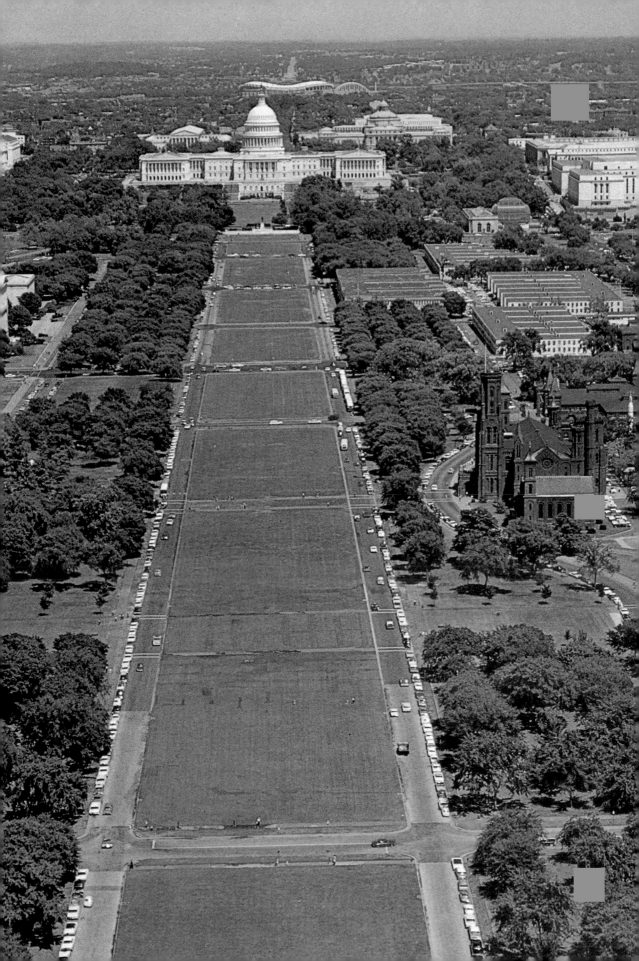

NORTH

Like a country manor, the White House sits in an 18-acre greensward in the heart of the city. Presidents from John Adams on have occupied this historic mansion. East and West Wings were added later to separate offices for the President and his staff from the crowded residence. The classic simplicity of the Treasury Building (right) and the ornate, rococo design of the multicolumned Executive Office Building (left) add architectural contrast to the setting.

To the north, across Pennsylvania Avenue, scene of Inaugural Parades, statue-studded Lafayette Square honors Andrew Jackson and foreign military leaders—Poland's Kosciusko, Germany's Von Steuben, and France's Rochambeau and Lafayette—who helped win the Nation's fight for independence.

Rescued from demolition by President and Mrs. John F. Kennedy, handsome historic homes around the park preserve its early 19th-century dignity. The

EMORY KRISTOF © N.G.S.

red brick home of Commodore Stephen
Decatur, completed in 1819 and now a
national historic landmark, will be fully
renovated. Its carriage house holds the
Truxton-Decatur Naval Museum, a valuable
collection of books, documents, relics, and
art related to naval history. Directly across
the park, Dolley Madison reigned as the
city's social arbiter after the death in 1836
of her husband President James Madison.

St. John's Episcopal Church, where many
Presidents have worshiped, is hidden
behind a screen of trees directly below the
scalloped roof of AFL-CIO headquarters at
center. St. Matthew's Cathedral (upper left),
scene of the funeral of President Kennedy,
lifts its green dome above a tide of business
buildings that sweeps northward.

Congressional statute and city zoning
laws prohibit private construction above
130 feet. The policy, originally derived
from fire safety standards, has helped
preserve a skyline dominated by the Capitol
and the Washington Monument.

WEST

Greek temple on the Potomac, the Lincoln Memorial commands a gateway to the Nation's Capital. Like the Washington Monument, the shrine to Abraham Lincoln grew out of decades of political and financial difficulties. Dedicated in 1922 at a cost of $3,045,400, the white marble structure, with its massive Doric columns, forms a fitting frame for the giant brooding figure of Lincoln inside.

The 2,000-foot-long Reflecting Pool and a smaller Rainbow Pool, with 142 fountains, stretch almost to the Monument's base. Until recently, temporary buildings erected by the Federal Government during World War II flanked the south side of the waterway. Others on the north still remain, despite President Franklin Roosevelt's determination to remove them immediately after the end of the war.

Spanning the Potomac River, the Arlington Memorial Bridge leads to the nearby Virginia shore. Beyond, the Avenue of Heroes, bearing the statue of Polar explorer Adm. Richard E. Byrd, continues to the gates of Arlington National Cemetery, where lie the Nation's honored dead. In the open expanse beneath the Custis-Lee Mansion (left), an eternal flame marks the grave of John F. Kennedy. A few hundred yards to the south, a single sentry paces in lonely cadence before the Tomb of the Unknowns.

A new bridge (far right) honoring Theodore Roosevelt arches above an island named for the conservation-minded President. The island was set aside as a bird sanctuary and memorial site.

EMORY KRISTOF © N.G.S.

SOUTH *Amid a man-made galaxy of automobile and street lights, the Jefferson Memorial lifts its curved dome above the Tidal Basin.*

Dedicated in 1943, the 200th anniversary of his birth, the gleaming white shrine to Thomas Jefferson stands only yards from the Potomac River.

The classical structure blends architectural styles of the Pantheon in Rome with Jefferson's own designs for the rotunda at the University of Virginia and his beloved home Monticello near Charlottesville, Virginia.

The monument's circular interior shelters a 19-foot bronze statue of the third American

EMORY KRISTOF © N.G.S.

President. Engraved inside the marble dome are his ringing words: "I have sworn upon the altar of God eternal hostility against every form of tyranny over the mind of man."

Early spring transforms the Tidal Basin into a flowery fantasy; hundreds of Japanese cherry trees lining its rim unfold their pink and white petals. During summer months, foot-powered paddle boats put out from the small dock (center, left) to carry visitors over placid, Potomac-fed waters.

Ribbons of light behind the memorial mark two of seven bridges linking the city to the Virginia shore.

WASHINGTON
FOR THE TOURIST

STATUTE MILE
0   1/2

■ Major tourist attractions
▫ Other points of interest
▫ Hotels and motels

Soundings in feet
+++++ Railroads
==== Roads under construction

NATIONAL GEOGRAPHIC SOCIETY ©

NW · NE
THE MALL — E. CAPITOL STREET
CAP·N. CAPITOL STREET
VIRGINIA
SW · SE
S. CAPITOL STREET

THE DISTRICT OF COLUMBIA IS DIVIDED INTO FOUR
SECTIONS BASED ON THE CAPITOL: NUMBERED AND
LETTERED STREETS BEGIN AT THE DIVIDING LINES

INDEX FOR MAJOR TOURIST ATTRACTIONS

Arlington National Cemetery D-E1
Bureau of Engraving and Printing ... D5
Capitol Building C7
Corcoran Gallery of Art B4
Federal Bureau of Investigation C5
Folger Library C8
House Office Buildings C7
Iwo Jima Statue C1

Jefferson Memorial D4
Kennedy Grave Site D1
Library of Congress C7-8
Lincoln Memorial C3
National Archives C6
National Geographic Society A4
Pan American Union C4
Pentagon E2
Senate Office Buildings C7
Smithsonian Institution
  Air and Space Building C5

Arts and Industries Building C5
Freer Gallery of Art C5
Museum of History and
  Technology C5
Museum of Natural History C5
National Gallery of Art C6
Smithsonian Building C5
Supreme Court C7-8
Tomb of the Unknowns E1
Washington Monument C4
White House B4

S. Capitol St. Bridge